GW00394320

FreeFrom all'Italiana with Anna Del Conte & Michelle Berriedale-Johnson

PRIMI

PRIMI
FreeFrom all'Italiana with Anna Del Conte
and Michelle Berriedale-Johnson
© Berrydales Books
ISBN 978-0-9518427-7-5

Published in 2017 by Berrydales Books
The right of Anne Del Conte and Michelle Berriedale-Johnson
to be identified as the authors of this work
has been asserted by them in accordance with the Copyright,
Designs and Patents Act 1988.

A CIP record of this book is available from the British Library.

All rights reserved. No part of this book may be reproduced, stored
in a retrieval system, or transmitted in any form or by any means,
electronic, mechanical, photocopying, recording or otherwise,
without the prior written permission of the copyright holder.

No responsibility for loss occasioned to any person acting or
refraining from action as a result of any material in this publication
can be accepted by the author or publisher.

Photographer: Ming Tang-Evans
Food Stylist: Rich Harris

Printed in the United Kingdom.

About the authors...

Photograph by Elena Heatherwick for
SUITCASE Magazine

Anna Del Conte has spent five decades writing about Italian food from the Renaissance to the twentieth century, and from the foothills of the Alps to tip of the Italian toe. Her many books are as authoritative a source as you will find on classic Italian food, and are not only a pleasure to cook from, but a delight to read.

At the age of 91, Anna could be excused for declining to experiment with the new gluten- and milk-free ingredients that are flooding the market, but on the contrary – she has taken up the challenge with a will.

The recipes that follow are a combination of classic recipes that are either naturally freefrom or have been adapted to be so – with new recipes designed for the many new, gluten-free pastas available.

Michelle Berriedale-Johnson has been involved with food allergy since the late 1980s, when her small son was diagnosed as milk intolerant. Since then she has manufactured freefrom foods, written more than a dozen books on allergy and freefrom, run an allergy magazine and now edits an extensive website – Foodsmatter.com – on food allergy and intolerance. She also runs the very successful FreeFrom Food Awards and FreeFrom Eating Out Awards, and is a regular speaker on allergy and the freefrom industry.

Anna and Michelle have been cooking together since they met in the 1980s over Cristoforo di Messisbugo's recipes which may, or may not, have been used at the court of Lucrezia Borgia in the early 1500s.

Contents

Key
GF: gluten-free
MF: milk-free
LF: lactose-free
LL: low-lactose

Please note the Sacla' sauces mentioned in this book
contain the following allergens:
Fiery Chilli Pesto: almonds, milk, sulphur dioxide
Free From Basil Pesto: soya, cashew nuts
Free From Tomato Pesto: soya
Truffle Pesto: cashew nuts, milk, egg
Wild Mushroom Risotto: soya

Introduction

Anna:

For a long time, Michelle kept asking me to write a book on gluten-free Italian food, but I refused because I didn't like the idea of having to exclude my beloved pasta from anything I wrote.

Then one day, Michelle sent me a large package. 'What is it?' I thought. I started unpacking, and out came bags and bags of different pasta: pasta made with rice flour, with cornflour, with beans… I was stunned, but I was even more stunned when I began to cook and eat them. 'Not bad,' I thought, 'not bad at all. Actually, some are very good.' I was hooked, and this book is the result.

In some of the recipes you will find that we suggest the use of Sacla' pesto or other Sacla' Free From sauces. As anybody who knows me and has read my books will know, I am not a cook who relies on any sort of prepared food – I like to make it all myself. But, sometimes even I am short of time, and I certainly know that many of my readers are often short of time. So I tried some of those….

I know that Sacla' sauces are all made in Italy. I have been to their factory in Asti many times and also tasted the raw products. I have also been to the fields where the basil for the Sacla' pesto is grown. They are on the border of Piedmont and Liguria, just the right spot to get the breeze from the sea, tempered by the drier climate of the inland.

There, under a huge walnut tree, we sat down to the most delicious *trofie al pesto alla* Genovese I have ever had. I was chatting to Sandra, one of the growers, and asked her if she makes her pesto in the mortar or in a food processor. She looked at me, laughed and said '*Ma, veramente*, I simply unscrew a jar of the pesto. It is just as good and it saves a lot of time.'

I feel this is the best accolade, and I leave the final judgement to you.

Michelle:

I have indeed been trying to persuade Anna to write a book about freefrom Italian cookery for years. So I am really delighted that she finally tried some of the very exciting gluten-free pastas now on the market – and that she actually liked them!

However, this book is not just about gluten-free, but also about the wider territory of freefrom. Freefrom lactose and milk products, yes, but also free from many others of those 14 major food allergens that need to be highlighted on all food products. We have only flagged the recipes as being free from gluten, milk or lactose, but in fact many of the recipes are also free of soya, egg, nuts, peanuts, sesame and mustard.

In fact, much Italian food is naturally freefrom. Polenta, made from corn or maize, and rice are as common in northern Italy as pasta; olive oil is used as often as butter as a cooking medium; while meat and fish dishes are usually simply prepared with herbs and vegetables, without the need for thickeners or cream. Nonetheless, pasta does remain the backbone of Italian cuisine outside Italy, so the development of good alternative, non-wheat-based pastas was crucial, if *freefrom all'Italiana* was ever really to take off.

Gluten-free pasta

You can now buy pasta made from a huge range of gluten-free ingredients: corn, rice, quinoa, buckwheat, soya beans, chickpeas, black beans, low-calorie konjac and even seaweed – although strictly speaking you do not make seaweed pasta at all, you just harvest it!

Some of these – especially corn and rice-based pasta – come very close to the texture and flavour of a durum wheat pasta; although of course, they will never taste exactly the same because the base ingredients are different. For some of the dishes in the book (such as the fennel and anchovy sauce on page 18), that is what you need: a relatively mild, smooth pasta that will not overpower the delicate flavour of the sauce.

Others – the pulse-based pasta, for example – can be coarser in texture and stronger in flavour, but that does not at all invalidate them as a base for a sauce. It just means that you have to devise different sauces that suit them, which is exactly what Anna has done.

Some, such as the konjac or seaweed, bear very little resemblance to classic pasta at all – they have much chewier and 'nyunkier' textures – but still make an excellent and unusual base for the right sauce.

Milk-free and lactose free

Confusingly, milk and lactose are not the same thing.

'Milk' on a food label refers to any milk-based food: milk itself, buttermilk, whey, cream, butter, yoghurt, cheese, ice cream and any food which uses any of these. If you have a problem with milk-based foods, you can be allergic – this means that you can have a potentially life-threatening immune system reaction to it. Or you can be intolerant, which means that you may feel ill – sometimes seriously ill – but it will not be life-threatening. Whichever it is, you need to avoid all milk-based products.

Although all animal milks share many characteristics, they are not identical, and there are some people who cannot tolerate cow's milk but can tolerate sheep's or goat's milk. Although parmesan is made from cow's milk, pecorino (used in several recipes) is a sheep's milk cheese, so those people who are only sensitive to cow's milk may be OK with it.

Lactose is the sugar is found in all animal milks, including human. If you are lactose intolerant it means that you do not make enough of the enzyme lactase to process that sugar; as a result it ferments in your gut. However, while there are relatively high levels of lactose sugar in 'straight' milk, as the milk is processed into butter, yoghurt or cheese so the lactose sugar is broken down by the fermentation process. The longer the cheese matures, the less lactose will remain. This means that really mature cheese such as parmesan or Pecorino Romano (the cheeses used almost exclusively in this book) will be suitable for someone on a low-lactose diet.

Pasta

Black bean spaghetti
with mussel sauce p.8

Chickpea or buckwheat pasta with garlic, olive oil and rosemary – Gluten-free/milk-free/lactose-free

Serves 4

400g chickpea or buckwheat fusilli or penne

7 tbsp extra virgin olive oil

4 garlic cloves, finely chopped

1–2 fresh chilli peppers, cores and seeds removed, finely chopped

2 rosemary sprigs, finely chopped

2 tsp lemon juice

Anna: *This is a robust, piquant sauce ideal for chickpea or buckwheat pasta. You might like to put in more chilli pepper or less. Taste it – careful, a tiny bit is quite enough – and decide for yourself.*

Michelle: *A great, simple and totally freefrom dish.*

Cook the pasta in plenty of well-salted, boiling water according to the instructions on the pack. While the pasta is cooking, heat the olive oil in a large frying pan. When hot, throw in the chopped garlic, chilli and rosemary and fry, stirring constantly for 1 minute, pressing the ingredients to release the juices.

Drain the pasta and turn it immediately into the frying pan. Now stir it over and over so that all the shapes can get thoroughly dressed.

Sprinkle with the lemon juice, stir again and serve at once, straight from the pan.

Bean or buckwheat pasta with broccoli sauce

Gluten-free/can be milk-free/low-lactose

Anna: *Broccoli sauce is a classic of southern Italian cooking and it is one of the best for chickpea pasta, although you certainly could use successfully with any other gluten-free pasta.*

Michelle: *This sauce is naturally gluten- and milk-free apart from the Pecorino Romano, which is optional anyhow. However, pecorino is made from sheep's milk, not cow's milk, so if you are only intolerant of cow's milk, you may be able to eat it. It is also a long-matured cheese, which means that it will be very low-lactose if you are lactose, not milk, intolerant.*

Serves 4

500g broccoli

400g gluten-free pasta, orecchiette would be excellent but, if not, penne)

5 tbsp extra virgin olive oil

3 garlic cloves, chopped

3 salted anchovies, boned and rinsed (or 6 anchovy fillets, drained), chopped

dried chilli, seeded and chopped

4 tbsp freshly grated Pecorino Romano (optional)

Cut the broccoli into small florets. Remove the outer layer of the stalks, and cut the stalks into small pieces. Wash and plunge them into a pan of rapidly boiling well-salted water. Cook until just tender, then lift them out of the water with a slotted spoon and put in a colander to drain; retain the cooking water to cook the pasta.

Cook the pasta in the broccoli stock, according to the instructions on the pack. If there is not enough stock to cook the pasta – you will need at least 3.5L of liquid – add boiling water and more salt.

Meanwhile, heat the olive oil in a large frying pan. Throw in the garlic, anchovies and chilli, and sauté for a minute or two, while pounding the ingredients down to release their flavour. Add the broccoli and fry gently for some 5 minutes, stirring frequently.

When cooked, drain the pasta and turn it immediately into the broccoli sauce. Stir on the heat for a good 2 minutes, and serve with a bowl of Pecorino Romano on the side, if you are using it.

Pasta salad with sun-dried tomato sauce

Gluten-free/milk-free/lactose-free

Serves 4

125g sun-dried tomatoes

1 tbsp red wine vinegar

1 tbsp balsamic vinegar

sea salt

8 tbsp extra virgin olive oil

1 tsp crushed chilli

3 garlic cloves, peeled and chopped

1 tbsp dried oregano

2 tbsp Sacla' Free From Tomato Pesto (contains soya)

400g gluten-free spaghetti

12 pitted black olives

Anna: *I am not particularly keen on pasta salad but I did love this sauce, which works particularly well with gluten-free pasta. I suggest one teaspoon of crushed chilli, but of course you can put less if you want to spare your palate from strong shocks (or more if you want to set your mouth on fire). Use plain olives, not the sort dressed with different flavourings.*

Michelle: *A splendidly naturally gluten-free and milk-free dish.*

Put the tomatoes in a bowl, pour over the red wine and balsamic vinegars, sprinkle with a pinch or two of salt, and leave them to reconstitute for at least 1 hour.

After that, drain the tomatoes, dry them with kitchen paper and coarsely chop them. Put them in a bowl and add 6 tablespoons of the olive oil, the chilli, garlic, ½ tablespoon of the oregano and the pesto. Mix well and set aside while you cook the pasta.

Cook the pasta in well-salted water according to the instructions on the pack. Drain and turn it immediately into the bowl with the tomatoes. Mix well and leave the pasta to cool. Do not refrigerate, because the salad should be served at room temperature.

Before serving, scatter the olives over the top, shower with the remaining ½ tablespoon of oregano, and pour over the remaining 2 tablespoons of olive oil.

Gluten-free spaghetti with tomato and anchovy sauce

Gluten-free/milk-free/lactose-free

Anna: *Most gluten-free pastas have a stronger flavour than wheat-based pastas, so they need good, strongly-flavoured sauces such as this.*

Michelle: *Agreed!*

Heat 4 tablespoons of the olive oil in a large frying pan and, when hot, throw in the garlic and anchovies. Sauté gently for about 2 minutes, squashing the anchovies down against the bottom of the pan to release the flavour.

Add the chilli, salt and tinned tomatoes. Turn the heat up and cook for 10 minutes, or until the sauce(d) has thickened, stirring frequently. Taste and adjust the salt and chilli to your liking.

Meanwhile, cook the pasta in plenty of well-salted boiling water according to the instructions on the pack. When cooked, drain the pasta, reserving a mugful of the cooking water. Tip the pasta straight into the frying pan with the sauce.

Stir on the heat for approximately 2 minutes, adding some of the reserved cooking water if necessary (some gluten-free pastas need more liquid than others). Pour over the remaining 2 tablespoons of olive oil. Sprinkle over the oregano and capers, and serve at once.

Variation: Instead of using the dried chilli, you could use Sacla' Fiery Chilli Pesto to give it more delicious heat. Just be aware that it does contain Pecorino Romano, so the recipe would no longer be milk-free, although it would be very low-lactose. (NB: this pesto also contains almonds and sulphur dioxide.)

Serves 4

6 tbsp extra virgin olive oil

4 garlic cloves, sliced

8 anchovy fillets, drained and chopped

½ tsp chilli flakes (more if you want it really hot)

pinch salt

1 x 400g and 1 x 225g tins chopped plum tomatoes

400g gluten-free spaghetti (brown rice spaghetti would work well)

1 tsp dried oregano

2 tbsp capers

Any gluten-free pasta with leek sauce

Gluten-free/can be milk-free

Serves 4

500g leeks, white part only
(NB: this is the weight of the leeks needed
for the sauce, not the whole leeks)

50g unsalted butter (or coconut oil for the
milk-free version)

4 tbsp olive oil

sea salt and freshly ground black pepper

150ml vegetable stock (a good, gluten-free
bouillon is fine)

¾ tsp turmeric

400g rice and maize fusilli

grated parmesan for the
table (optional)

Anna: *Leeks are quite popular in northern Italy, but are not often made into a pasta sauce. However, because I like them very much I created this sauce in which I have used turmeric – very non-Italian! I used this with a rice and maize flour fusilli.*

Michelle: *Anna maintains that the flavour of the butter is crucial for this dish, so she was reluctant to allow me to suggest using olive oil, or even a milk-free spread or coconut oil. However, if you want to try this, just use an extra two tablespoons of coconut oil instead of the butter – but remember that it will not taste quite as Anna intended (although you might like it even more!). Remember that if you are lactose, rather than milk, intolerant, you may be able to eat the parmesan.*

Preheat the oven to 100C/fan 80C/gas mark ¼

Cut the leeks into very thin rounds, put them in a sink of water and wash very well. Scoop the leeks up and place in a colander to drain.

Heat 25g of the butter and all of the olive oil in a large sauté pan. When the butter foam begins to subside, add the leeks a little at a time, so that you can coat them in the fat more easily.

When all the leeks are in the pan, add a generous pinch of salt and cook over a lively heat for 2–3 minutes, while you stir the whole time. Pour in about half the stock, mix well and cover the pan with a lid.

Cook for some 30 minutes, turning the leeks over occasionally and adding a little more stock if necessary. After 15 minutes, season with the turmeric and plenty of pepper, mix thoroughly and continue cooking until the leeks are totally mashed – a liquid sauce of a lovely yellowy-green colour. Taste and adjust the seasoning.

Meanwhile, cook the pasta in plenty of well-salted boiling water according to the instructions on the pack. While the pasta is cooking, put the remaining 25g of butter in a heatproof serving bowl and place the bowl in the oven.

When the pasta is ready, drain and turn it immediately into the warmed bowl, mix very thoroughly with the butter, spoon over the sauce and serve with a bowl of parmesan on the side.

Black bean spaghetti with mussel sauce

Gluten-free/milk-free/lactose-free

Serves 4

400g black bean spaghetti

1kg fresh mussels in their shells, or 500g frozen mussels

If you are using fresh mussels:

1 lemon, cut in half

3 garlic cloves, squashed and peeled

3 tbsp extra virgin olive oil

For the sauce:

1 tbsp olive oil

1 clove garlic, peeled and crushed

½ tsp flaked chilli (or more according to taste)

3 tbsp flatleaf parsley, chopped

1 tbsp Sacla' Free From Basil Pesto (contains soya and cashew nuts)

150ml white wine

a squeeze or two of lemon juice

sea salt

Anna: *We used this sauce to dress black bean spaghett and decided it was perfect, but it is such a good sauce that we are sure it would work well with any other gluten-free pasta.*

Michelle: *Pulse-based pastas are now becoming quite common. They tend to have a rather different, coarser texture than wheat, corn or rice-based pasta and a fairly vigorous flavour, so are best matched with strong-flavoured sauces such as this. If pushed for time, you could use frozen mussels – although the flavour will not be quite as good, it will still be pretty spectacular.*

First prepare the fresh mussels or defrost the frozen mussels, reserving their juices.

For the fresh mussels:

Mussels these days are usually sold already clean; if not, wash them in a sink of cold water, scrubbing them hard, removing barnacles and beard. Remove and throw away any mussel which remains open when you tap it on a hard surface – that means that it is dead. Put the lemon halves, 3 garlic cloves and 3 tablespoons of olive oil in a large sauté pan with a tight fitting lid, add the mussels and put the lid on the pan.

Put the pan on a high heat and cook for 4–5 minutes, shaking it occasionally to allow all the mussels to get in touch with the bottom of the pan. All the mussels should be open by now. As soon as they are cool enough to touch, remove the flesh from the shells, letting the lovely juices fall back into the pan.

Put the cooked mussels in a bowl and discard the shells, garlic and the lemon. Have a look at the juices. If there is some grit at the bottom of the pan, strain the juices through a fine sieve. Nowadays mussels are mostly farmed, so not very dirty; this step is not often necessary. Set the mussels aside while you cook the pasta and make the sauce.

To make the sauce:

Cook the pasta in plenty of well-salted boiling water according to the instructions on the pack.

While the pasta is cooking, put the sauté pan back on the heat with 1 tablespoon olive oil. Heat it and add the garlic, chilli and 2 tablespoons of the parsley. Fry for 1 minute and as soon as the garlic aroma rises, add the pesto, mussel juices and wine. Boil briskly for a couple of minutes to reduce the juices by approximately one-third.

Turn the mussels into the pan, reduce the heat and cook very gently for a minute to heat the mussels through in the sauce without letting them break up.

When the pasta is ready, drain and turn it into a warmed serving bowl. Spoon the mussels and sauce over the top, sprinkle with the remaining 1 tablespoon parsley and squeeze over the lemon juice. Serve immediately.

Any gluten-free pasta with fennel sauce

Gluten-free/milk-free/lactose-free

Serves 4

1–2 fennel bulbs, about 400g

120ml extra virgin olive oil

6 anchovy fillets,
drained and chopped

2 garlic cloves, chopped

sea salt and freshly ground
black pepper

1 tbsp fennel seeds

400g any rice or
corn-based penne or fusilli

12 black olives, pitted

Anna: *A delicious sauce with any pasta – we are sure you will love it.*

Michelle: *Too right – and naturally freefrom!*

Cut the feathery fronds off the stalks and reserve. Cut the stalks off the fennel bulb then throw the stalks away. Cut the bulb in quarters lengthwise, and then into thin strips. Wash under cold water and then leave in a colander to drain.

Take a large sauté pan with a lid and pour in about half of the olive oil. Add the anchovies and garlic and sauté for a minute or two, while pressing the mixture down with a fork against the bottom of the pan to release the juices. Remove as much of the anchovy and garlic from the oil as you can, and set aside.

Throw the fennel into the pan, a little at a time, so that all the pieces of fennel can absorb some of the garlicky oil. When all the fennel is in the pan, cook over a lively heat for some 5 minutes, turning the fennel over and over.

Add a generous pinch of salt and 2 tablespoons of hot water. Turn down the heat and cover the pan. Cook very slowly until the fennel is very tender, so tender that you can mush it up with a fork – it will take at least half an hour. Keep an eye on the sauce during the cooking; you will have to add a few extra tablespoons of hot water two or three times during the cooking. The fennel should be cooking all the time in quite a bit of liquid.

While the fennel is cooking, put the fennel seeds in a mortar and pound them with a pestle until broken up. Add to the fennel sauce together with a generous grating of pepper. Mix well, taste and adjust the salt.

Meanwhile, cook the pasta in plenty of well-salted boiling water according to the instructions on the pack.

Drain the pasta, reserving a cupful of the cooking water. Tip the pasta into the fennel sauce. Add the reserved chopped garlic and anchovies and the remaining olive oil and mix very well, adding some of the pasta water to loosen the sauce.

Spoon the pasta into a warmed bowl and keep it warm while you chop the reserved fennel tops. Sprinkle these over the top of the pasta, throw in the black olives and serve.

Smoked salmon and pesto sauce for any gluten-free pasta

Gluten-free/milk-free/lactose-free

Serves 4

400g brown rice spaghetti, or approximately 80g seaweed 'spaghetti' or 'tagliatelle' (NB: seaweed swells up to five times its size when cooked).

8 tbsp/1.5 jars of Sacla' Free From Basil Pesto (contains soya and cashew nuts)

300g smoked salmon

4 tbsp extra virgin olive oil

sea salt and freshly ground black pepper

Anna: *My Italian daughter-in-law gave me this delicious sauce when I was staying with her and my son. Smoked salmon is one of the few foreign foods that are now part of the Italian food scene: it is eaten usually with green salad, but it is also combined with Italian ingredients, as in this sauce. We used Sacla' Free From Basil Pesto because this sauce does not need any cheese. You can also be more adventurous and use either a vegetable spiralizer or – our preference – seaweed spaghetti or tagliatelle. These will have a chewier texture than any pasta, but are rather delicious and certainly unusual.*

Michelle: *Simple, delicious and totally, naturally freefrom. I love the idea of using seaweed: not only super-healthy, but absolutely on trend – just where freefrom ought to be!*

Cook the pasta in plenty of well-salted boiling water according to the instructions on the back. If you are using the seaweed 'spaghetti' or 'tagliatelle' you will need to boil it for 10–15 minutes. It will never get as soft as pasta, but should be just pleasantly chewy.

While the pasta is cooking, put the pesto in a large, heatproof serving bowl and place the bowl in a warm oven at 100°C (212°F/fan 80°C/Gas ¼). Next, cut the salmon into short strips.

When the pasta is cooked, drain, reserving a mugful of the cooking water, and turn it into the warm bowl. Add the olive oil, half of the salmon and enough of the pasta water to loosen the sauce.

Season with a good grinding of pepper, taste and add salt if necessary. Mix very well using two forks to lift the strands up in the air, scatter the remaining salmon over the top, and serve.

Egg and cheese pasta bake
Gluten-free

Serves 4

400g buckwheat penne or fusilli

70g unsalted butter (and extra butter for greasing the dish)

2 tsp Vecon or other gluten-free yeast spread (not Marmite, which is not truly gluten-free)

2 eggs, lightly mixed together

250ml double cream

50g Grana Padano, coarsely grated

50g Gruyère, coarsely grated

a generous grating of nutmeg

sea salt and freshly ground black pepper

a handful of gluten-free breadcrumbs

Anna: *In this dish the pasta is finished off in the oven to form a delicious crust on the top. It is a perfect dish if you want to cook your supper in advance, as it gives you time to sit down and relax with a glass of wine before you eat. We used a buckwheat pasta for this recipe, but it would go well with any other grain-based pasta (but not a pulse-based one).*

Michelle: *This dish, which is delicious, is so dependent on butter and cheese that it is not really viable to substitute them. Apologies to those of you who do not eat milk products...*

Preheat the oven to 200°C (400°F/fan 180°C/Gas 6).

Cook the pasta in plenty of well-salted water according to the instructions on the pack.

While the pasta is cooking, melt the butter in a small saucepan, add the Vecon and cook gently, stirring the whole time until everything has melted together.

In a separate bowl, beat the eggs together with the cream, then mix in the two cheeses, nutmeg and salt and pepper to taste.

When the pasta is ready, drain it, reserving a mugful of the cooking water. Tip the pasta back into the pan and toss it immediately with the butter, adding some of the reserved water to make sure the sauce coats the pasta well.

Butter the oven dish and sprinkle with the dried gluten-free breadcrumbs. Tip in the pasta and spoon the egg mixture over the top.

Bake for 10–15 minutes, or until a lovely golden crust has formed on the top, and serve.

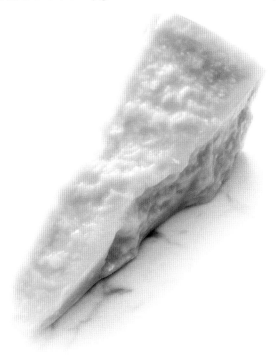

Mushrooms and anchovies pasta bake

Gluten-free/milk-free/lactose-free

Serves 4

15g dried porcini mushrooms

350g brown mushrooms

8 tbsp extra virgin olive oil
(with extra oil for greasing the dish)

2 garlic cloves, chopped

2 anchovy fillets, drained

rind of 1 unwaxed lemon and juice of ½ lemon

sea salt and freshly ground black pepper

50g dried gluten-free breadcrumbs

2 tbsp chopped flatleaf parsley

a pinch or two of chilli flakes

400g any gluten-free penne or fusilli

1 tbsp Sacla' Free From Basil Pesto
(contains soya and cashew nuts)

gluten-free breadcrumbs

Preheat the oven to 180C (375°F/fan 160°C/Gas 4).

Anna: *This is one of the most successful pasta bakes the made – easy to prepare, and even easier to eat!*

Michelle: *And totally freefrom!*

Preheat the oven to 180°C (375°F/fan 160°C/Gas 4).

Soak the porcini in a bowl of hot water for 20 minutes. When the time is up, drain the porcini, keeping the liquid, and chop them coarsely.

While the porcini are soaking, clean the mushrooms and slice them (if they are large, cut them in half and slice). Heat 4 tablespoons of the olive oil in a large frying pan, add the garlic and anchovies and sauté gently, pounding the mixture in the bottom of the pan.

Now throw in the brown mushrooms and fry them over a lively heat, while turning them to make sure they get coated in the oil. After 5 minutes, add the drained porcini and continue to fry for a further 5 minutes.

Add the lemon juice, salt and pepper and turn the heat down. Cook gently for about 10 minutes, adding some more of the porcini liquid whenever the sauce gets too dry.

Heat the remaining oil in a clean frying pan and, when hot, throw in the gluten-free breadcrumbs and lemon rind. Fry for 2 minutes, or until the crumbs are golden, stirring the whole time. Then add the parsley and chilli and continue to fry for 30 seconds.

Meanwhile, cook the pasta in plenty of well-salted boiling water according to the instructions on pack. Drain and tip it immediately into the mushroom sauce, then add the pesto. Stir constantly over a gentle heat for a minute or two. Oil a large shallow oven dish and sprinkle with gluten-free breadcrumbs. Tip in the pasta, spread it out to cover the bottom of the dish, then spoon the fried breadcrumb mixture over the top.

Bake for 15 minutes. Allow to rest for a couple of minutes before serving.

Rice

Tomatoes stuffed with
rice and potatoes p.25

Risotto with Jerusalem artichokes
Gluten-free

Serves 4

400g Jerusalem artichokes

1.5–1.75 litres gluten-free chicken or vegetable stock

50g unsalted butter

2 tbsp olive oil

2 tbsp onion, chopped

sea salt

400g Italian rice (eg Arborio, Carnaroli, Vialone Nano)

4 tbsp dry sherry, such as Manzanilla

2 tsp Sacla' Truffle Pesto (contains milk, cashew nuts and egg)

50g Parmigiano Reggiano, grated

freshly ground black pepper

Anna: *I don't peel Jerusalem artichokes (too difficult); I scrub them very vigorously with a hard brush under running water. Sacla' Truffle Pesto, which is quite delicious, is a perfect complement to Jerusalem artichokes.*

Michelle: *The butter, truffle pesto and parmesan are crucial to this dish, so it would be difficult to create a milk-free version without changing it dramatically.*

Wash and scrub the Jerusalem artichokes and cut them into small cubes. Heat the stock and keep it at nearly boiling point all the time while you make the risotto. Heat half the butter and all of the olive oil in your risotto pan – a deep sauté pan is perfect. Throw in the onion, sprinkle with a pinch of salt and sauté for a good 7–8 minutes until it is soft and golden, but not brown.

Add the Jerusalem artichokes and continue frying gently for 5 minutes, stirring the vegetable dice around in the fatty onion. Now add the rice, mix with the vegetables and sauté for 2–3 minutes until the grains are translucent and well coated with fat. Pour in the sherry and boil briskly to evaporate.

Now you must begin to add the stock, one ladleful at a time (about 150ml). Add the first ladleful, mix well and continue cooking. When all the stock has been absorbed by the rice, add another ladleful and continue until the rice is cooked (good Italian rice cooks in about 18–20 minutes, depending on the variety).

You might not need all the stock; on the other hand if you have no more stock left, just add boiling water. It is difficult to state the exact quantity of liquid necessary, since it depends on the variety of the rice. When the rice is *al dente* – or cooked as you like it – mix in the Sacla' Truffle Pesto and remove the pan from the heat.

Add the remaining butter and cheese. Turn the heat off. Put the lid on the pan and let the risotto rest for 2 minutes, before you give it a final energetic stir. Grind over some black pepper, and bring it to the table.

Risotto with asparagus

Gluten-free/can be milk-free/can be low-lactose

Serves 4

350g asparagus

2 litres gluten-free chicken or vegetable stock

75g unsalted butter

2 shallots, finely chopped

350g Italian rice (eg Arborio, Carnaroli,
Vialone Nano)

2 tbsp white vermouth

sea salt and freshly ground black pepper

100g freshly grated Parmigiano Reggiano

Anna: *This is one of the most deliciously delicate risotti I know. Some cooks add two tablespoons of cream at the end of the cooking, but I prefer to stick to the traditional butter.*

Michelle: *Risotto should always be cooked with butter rather than oil, as the rice does not absorb the oil. The butter will also give a very specific and delicate flavour to the dish. However, if you want to make the dish totally milk-free, substitute three tablespoons of a light olive oil for the butter, and leave out the parmesan. Or if you are just avoiding lactose, use olive oil, but you may be able to use the parmesan.*

Wash and trim the asparagus, cut off the hard stalks, and put in a saucepan with the stock and bring to the boil. Boil for 15 minutes. (NB: you are cooking the hard stalks in the stock to give it flavour; you will not be using them in the dish.)

Scoop out and discard the stalks, and keep the stock nearly boiling for the whole of the cooking time, since you must add simmering liquid to the rice. Cut the tender part of the asparagus into 1.5–2 cm pieces, set aside the spear tops. Heat half the butter, add the shallots and sauté gently until soft. Add the asparagus pieces, but not the spears. Sauté gently for 5 minutes, stirring constantly, then add the rice.

Continue cooking until the grains appear translucent and well coated with the butter. Splash with the vermouth, cook for a minute or two, then begin to add the stock one ladleful at a time. When the rice looks dry, add another ladleful and then another ladleful until the rice is cooked. If you have finished all the stock and the rice is not cooked to your liking, simply add extra boiling water.

About 5 minutes before the rice is ready (good Italian rice takes about 18–20 minutes to cook, depending on the variety), add the top spears and salt and pepper to taste. When the rice is done, turn off the heat, add the remaining butter and half the Parmigiano Reggiano, cover the pan and leave the risotto to rest for 2 minutes. Stir energetically and bring to the table with a bowl of the remaining Parmigiano Reggiano on the side.

Risotto with spinach

Gluten-free/milk-free/lactose-free

Anna: *You can make this risotto milk-free by simply replacing the butter with six tablespoons of olive oil. It is just as delicious, although with a slightly different flavour.*

Michelle: *Yes, it is!*

Serves 4

1.25 litres gluten-free vegetable stock

either 75g unsalted butter and 1 tbsp olive oil or 6 tbsp olive oil

1 small onion, chopped

500g cooked spinach (or frozen spinach leaf, defrosted)

350g Italian rice (eg Arborio, Carnaroli, Vialone Nano)

150ml dry white wine

6 anchovy fillets, drained (or 3 anchovies preserved in salt, cleaned and washed)

1 garlic clove

sea salt and freshly ground black pepper

Heat the stock and keep it just simmering for the whole time that you cook the rice. Using your hands, squeeze any liquid out of the spinach.

Heat the butter and olive oil (or just the oil) in your risotto pan. When the butter is turning a hazelnut colour, throw in the onion and sauté for 5–6 minutes. Add the spinach and continue to sauté for a few more minutes, turning the whole mixture over and over.

Now add the rice and fry it over a lively heat until all the grains become translucent. Splash with the wine and let it evaporate over high heat for a minute or two.

Add the first ladleful of hot stock and, when the rice has absorbed all the liquid, pour in another ladleful of stock. Go on cooking in this way until the rice is nearly done (good Italian rice takes 18–20 minutes to cook).

Chop together the anchovy fillets and garlic, and mix into the risotto, adding salt and pepper to taste. Mix well and continue cooking until the rice is done the way you like, and then serve.

Tomatoes stuffed with rice and potatoes

Gluten-free/milk-free/lactose-free

Anna: *Dishes of lusciously coloured, stuffed vegetables are one of the joys of Italian cooking, and always among them are tomatoes. Try to get the big knobby tomatoes, which have more flavour.*

Michelle: *Another delicious, naturally freefrom dish!*

Serves 6

- large ripe but firm tomatoes, each weighing about 200g

- ea salt and freshly ground black pepper

- pinch of flaked chilli

- 0g uncooked Italian rice (eg Arborio, Carnaroli, Vialone Nano)

- tbsp extra virgin olive oil (with extra or greasing the dish)

- garlic clove, chopped

- anchovy fillets, rinsed and chopped

- tbsp flatleaf parsley, chopped

- tbsp Sacla' Free From Tomato Pesto (contains soya)

- large potatoes, cut into very small cubes

- tsp dried oregano

Heat the oven to 180°C (375°F/fan 160°C/Gas 4).

Cut the top from each tomato and reserve. Scoop the flesh and seeds out of the tomatoes, discard some of the seeds, chop the flesh into small pieces, and place it with the pulp in a bowl with a pinch of salt and the flaked chilli.

Add the rice, 3 tablespoons of the olive oil, garlic, anchovies, parsley and tomato pesto. Mix thoroughly. Taste and adjust the seasoning to your liking.

Sprinkle the inside of the tomatoes with salt and fill them with the mixture. 'Lid' with the reserved tomato tops. Put the tomatoes in an oiled ovenproof dish into which they will fit comfortably, but not too loosely.

Put the cubed potato in a bowl, spoon over 1 tablespoon of the remaining olive oil and mix well to coat all the cubes, then arrange them around the tomatoes in the dish. Shower with the remaining 1 tablespoon of oil and oregano. Cook for about 1½ hours or until the potato and rice are cooked, and serve.

Mushroom risotto

Gluten-free/can be milk-free/can be low-lactose

Serves 4

15g dried porcini

1.2 litres gluten-free vegetable stock or light chicken stock

3 tbsp olive oil

½ onion, very finely chopped

1 celery stalk, very finely chopped

1 garlic clove, very finely chopped

6 parsley sprigs, very finely chopped

1 tbsp tomato purée

sea salt and freshly ground black pepper

250g brown mushrooms, cleaned and sliced

50g unsalted butter

350g Italian rice (eg Arborio, Carnaroli, Vialone Nano)

150ml dry white wine

freshly grated parmesan

Anna: *There are as many risotti con funghi in northern Italy as there are cooks. This is one of my most used recipes, good and quite simple. I alway add some dry porcini for added flavour Sacla' makes a wild mushroom sauce that works very well here if you'd like to save some time; simply use it instead of the mushrooms and porcini.*

Michelle: *Again, Anna would rather tha you used butter for this dish, but if you do not eat milk products, substitute two tablespoons of olive oil for the butter when you cook the rice, and leave out the parmesan.*

Variation: 1 jar of Sacla' Free From Wild Mushroom Risotto (contains soya) instead of the mushrooms and the porcini.

To make the mushroom sauce:

Put the dried porcini in a bowl, cover with boiling water and set aside for about 20 minutes. (If you are using the ready-made Sacla' sauce, you do not need to do this.) Heat the stock and keep it just simmering all through the cooking of the rice.

Heat the olive oil with the onion in a frying pan and cook gently for 2–3 minutes. Add the celery, garlic and parsley and sauté gently until the vegetables are soft, stirring very frequently. Stir in the tomato purée and fry for a minute, then pour in a little stock. Continue cooking for about 5 minutes.

making the mushroom sauce:

Remove the dried porcini from the liquid. Rinse them under cold water and dry them well. Chop them and add to the pan with a little more stock. Season with salt and pepper, and cook for about 2–3 minutes. Add the brown mushrooms and cook over high heat for a few minutes, then turn down the heat and continue cooking for a further 15 minutes, adding a little stock if there is no liquid in the pan. Set aside and keep warm.

For the ready-made sauce:

Tip the sauce into the pan with the celery, garlic and parsley, and cook gently for 3–5 minutes. Set aside and keep warm.

For the rice:

Melt the butter (or heat the olive oil) in a heavy-bottomed saucepan. Add the rice and toast it for a minute or so, stirring constantly. Splash with the wine and let it evaporate while you continue stirring. Now add the simmering stock a ladleful at a time, letting the liquid be absorbed by the rice before you add the next. If the rice is still not cooked but all the stock has been used, just add boiling water.

When the rice is cooked to your satisfaction, spoon in 2 or 3 tablespoons of the mushroom sauce, mix well and transfer the risotto to a warmed bowl or to warmed individual plates. Spoon the remaining mushroom sauce over the risotto, and serve at once with a bowl of grated parmesan on the side.

Bean and vegetable risotto soup

Gluten-free/milk-free/lactose-free

Serves 5–6

200g dried borlotti or
cannellini beans

1 knuckle of unsmoked
bacon or ham

1 bay leaf

1½ onions, chopped

1 medium carrot, diced

1 celery stick, diced

2 to 3 cabbage leaves, shredded

40g olive oil

1 garlic clove, finely chopped

1 small rosemary sprig, chopped

150g coarse grain pure gluten-free pork sausage,
skinned and crumbled

300g Italian rice (eg Arborio, Carnaroli, Vialone Nano)

100ml red wine

1 tbsp tomato purée

sea salt and freshly ground black pepper

Anna: *This is a very rich, soupy risotto that must be made with dried beans and not tinned ones, because you need the flavour of the liquid in which they have cooked.*

Michelle: *Another excellent naturally freefrom dish. If you can think far enough ahead to soak your beans overnight, this is not a hard-work dish. It just involves a lot of soaking and boiling – but it is very much worth it!*

Soak the beans overnight in cold water. Drain and rinse.

Put the beans, knuckle of bacon, bay leaf, two-thirds of the onion, carrot, celery and cabbage leaves in a heavy-bottomed saucepan. Cover with about 2 litres of cold water and bring slowly to the boil. Simmer, covered, for about 3 hours (this can be done one or two days in advance; cool and chill until you are ready to use it).

Leaving the soup to simmer, lift the ham or bacon knuckle out and remove the meat from the bone. Cut the meat into small pieces. Remove the bay leaf and discard.

Put the meat, oil, garlic, rosemary, sausage and the remaining onion in a clean saucepan and fry gently for 5 minutes, stirring frequently. Add the rice and mix well. Pour over the wine, boil briskly for 1 or 2 minutes, then add the tomato purée. Pour over 200ml of the simmering soup and stir over a moderate heat. When the rice has absorbed nearly all the liquid, add another 150ml of the soup. Keep stirring the rice, adding more soup as the rice dries out, but do not add too much soup at a time.

When the rice is cooked *al dente*, strain the soup and add any beans or pieces of vegetables left over in the stockpot, but do not add any more liquid – this risotto should be rather liquid. Taste, season with salt and pepper, and serve.

Oven-baked risotto

Gluten-free/can be milk-free/low-lactose

Serves 4

1 or 2 shallots, or 1 small onion, finely chopped

3 tbsp olive oil

1 garlic clove, chopped

½ celery stick, chopped

½ carrot, chopped

250g minced lean pork

100ml dry white wine

500ml gluten-free meat stock (or 1 gluten-free meat bouillon cube dissolved in 500ml water)

300g Italian rice (eg Arborio, Carnaroli, Vialone Nano)

25g butter (or 1 tbsp olive oil)

4 tbsp freshly grated parmesan

sea salt and freshly ground black pepper

Anna: *This is an odd hybrid dish, part-risotto, part-oven-cooked rice. The result is delicious.*

Michelle: *To make this dish milk-free, use one table-spoon of oil instead of the butter, and leave out the parmesan. If you are just avoiding lactose, you may be able to eat the parmesan as it is very low-lactose.*

Gently sauté the shallots in the olive oil until soft. Add the garlic, celery and carrot, and cook for 7 minutes, stirring frequently.

Mix in the pork and brown well. Splash with the wine, stir, then pour over about 125ml of the stock. Cover the pan and simmer for about 1 hour, stirring every now and then and adding a little more stock if necessary. Heat the oven to 200°C (400°F/fan 180°C/Gas 6).

Cook the rice in salted boiling water for 7–8 minutes. Drain and add to the meat together with the remaining stock. Bring to the boil, then add the butter (or oil) and parmesan. Mix thoroughly and transfer to a buttered or oiled ovenproof dish.

Bake for 15–20 minutes or so until a light crust is formed on the top. Serve with a bowl of parmesan on the side.

Rice with peas

Gluten-free/can be milk-free/
low-lactose

Serves 4

1 kg sugar snap peas (in their pods)

2 tbsp olive oil

50g unsalted butter

1 banana shallot, very finely chopped

2 tbsp flatleaf parsley, chopped

1 tsp sugar

300g Italian rice (eg Arborio, Carnaroli, Vialone Nano)

1 litre gluten-free chicken or vegetable stock

sea salt and freshly ground black pepper

1 tbsp fennel seeds, crushed

50g freshly grated parmesan

Anna: *Neither a soup nor a risotto, this is one of the traditional dishes of the Veneto, where the peas are very small. Here we found sugar snap peas are the best variety to use.*

Michelle: *To make this dish milk-free, substitute an extra two tablespoons of oil for the butter, and leave out the parmesan. If you are just avoiding lactose you may be able to eat the parmesan, as it is very low-lactose.*

First, pod the sugar snap peas, keeping the pods and the peas separate. Wash the pods, put them in the saucepan, and add 1.5 litres of water and 2 tsp of salt. Bring to the boil and cook until the pods are very tender. Drain, reserving the liquid.

Put the pods in a food processor and process to a purée. Measure out 1 litre of the cooking liquid, and add it to the purée. Put the mixture into a saucepan and bring slowly to the boil.

Meanwhile, put the oil, butter and shallot in a heavy-bottomed saucepan and sauté until the shallot is pale golden and soft. Mix in half the parsley, peas and sugar. Cook over a low heat for 2 minutes, stirring constantly.

Add the rice and cook, stirring constantly for 2 minutes, then pour in the stock and the pod purée.

Season with the fennel seeds, salt and a good grinding of pepper. Cook, covered, until the rice is cooked (good Italian rice cooks in about 18–20 minutes, depending on the variety).

Turn off the heat and mix in the parmesan. Taste and adjust the seasoning. Ladle the soup into individual bowls and sprinkle with the parsley. Serve immediately.

Risotto with prawns and peas

Gluten-free/can be milk-free

Serves 4

50g unsalted butter

2 tbsp olive oil

3 banana shallots, finely chopped

sea salt and black pepper

1.2 litres fish stock (or 2 gluten-free fish stock cubes dissolved in 1.2 litres water)

300g Italian rice (eg Arborio, Carnaroli, Vialone Nano)

1½ tsp gluten-free curry powder, medium strength

3 tbsp dry sherry

150g frozen petits pois

300g frozen prawns

1–2 tsp lemon juice, to taste

Anna: *A delicious and nourishing dish that you could produce at the last minute with ingredients you have in your freezer. Buy the best frozen prawns you can find – they have more flavour. The rest is easy.*

Michelle: *If you want the risotto to be milk-free as well, eliminate the butter and use six tablespoons of olive oil in total.*

In a large and heavy saucepan, heat the butter and olive oil (or all of the oil) until the butter begins to turn golden. Throw in the shallots and cook over moderate heat for 2–3 minutes. Sprinkle with some salt and continue cooking on a lower heat until the shallot is soft – another 4–5 minutes – stirring frequently.

Put the stock in a saucepan and bring to the boil. Keep it on the lowest possible heat all through the cooking of the rice.

Add the rice to the shallots and sauté for 1–2 minutes while stirring constantly, so that all the grains absorb some of the fat. Sprinkle with the curry powder, cook for a further minute, then splash with the sherry.

Cook, stirring constantly, until the sherry has been absorbed, then begin to pour in the stock a ladleful at a time, as with all the risottos. Do not add more liquid until the rice is beginning to get dry. If you finish the fish stock before the rice is properly cooked, just add boiling water.

About 10 minutes after you have begun adding the stock, throw in the petits pois. Mix well and cook for 5 minutes, then add the prawns and mix thoroughly. Season but be careful with the salt, because the fish stock might be already salted, and the prawns certainly are.

Cook until the rice is ready (good Italian rice cooks in about 18–20 minutes, depending on the variety).

Mix in the lemon juice, taste and adjust the seasoning. Serve at once.

Rice and courgette torta

Gluten-free/low-lactose

Serves 4

500g courgettes, cut into matchsticks

3 banana shallots, thinly sliced

170g Italian rice (eg Arborio, Carnaroli, Vialone Nano)

100ml extra virgin olive oil (with extra for greasing the tin)

3 eggs

6 tbsp freshly grated Parmigiano Reggiano

a pinch of saffron strands

1 tsp of caster sugar

sea salt and freshly ground black pepper

150ml gluten-free vegetable stock

Anna: *This is delicious hot or at room temperature, but neither straight from the oven nor the fridge. We served it with green salad and it was perfect; a tomato salad dressed with olive oil and lemon juice would be very good too. The torta is very good made with leeks instead of courgettes (in this case, eliminate the shallots and increase the quantity of the leeks to 750g).*

Michelle: *The torta does depend heavily on Parmigiano Reggiano for its flavour, so it would be hard to leave it out but, if you are lactose rather than milk intolerant you may be able to eat it anyhow as the parmesan is very low-lactose.*

Put the courgettes, shallots and rice in a bowl. Add the olive oil and mix thoroughly, using two forks: they are better than spoons for amalgamating the various ingredients.

In a separate, small bowl, lightly beat the eggs together, mix in the cheese, and add to the bowl with the rice mixture. Mix thoroughly.

Put the saffron strands in a mortar, add the sugar and pound with the pestle until the saffron is all broken up. Using a pastry brush, add it to the rice mixture (a pastry brush will get the saffron out of the bowl more easily than a spoon will). Pour ½ tablespoon of hot water into the mortar, shake the water around and then pour it into the bowl with the rice – saffron is more precious than gold dust, you don't want to waste any.

Mix the whole thing very thoroughly with the two forks, and season with salt and pepper. Then cover the bowl with a cloth and set aside for about two hours, but remember to mix every now and then, so that all the rice gets the chance to soak and soften in the liquid.

Preheat the oven to 180°C (375°F/fan 160°C/Gas 4).

Oil an 18cm springform cake tin, line with parchment paper, then oil the paper. Spoon the mixture into the tin, cover and bake for about 70 minutes until the rice is cooked – you can scrape a few grains and taste. About halfway through the cooking time, pour the stock onto the top of the dish, allowing it to soak in.

Leave the torta in the tin for about 5 minutes, then unmould, peel off the paper and serve.

Polenta and pulses

Lentils with sausage
and mushroom p.42

Polenta with Gorgonzola sauce

Gluten-free

Anna: *Polenta, is of course, by definition gluten-free as it is corn. Classic polenta is delicious but both time-consuming and hard work to make, so these days most people buy polenta istantanea (quick cook, instant or pre-cooked polenta), which can be made in five minutes flat. Not, maybe, quite as good as a classic polenta, but pretty OK – especially with a good sauce. I originally created this sauce for a dish of tagliatelle. When we decided to write this gluten-free book we decided it could go equally well with polenta. We tried it and liked it. Now you try it!*

Michelle: *I did try it – and it is delicious! It is, however, so dependent on the cheese and butter for its flavour that you cannot really make it milk-free.*

Serves 4

250g quick cook/instant polenta

30g unsalted butter

6 fresh sage leaves

1 garlic clove, peeled and sliced

100g Gorgonzola

150ml double cream

freshly ground black pepper

First, make the polenta by following the instructions on the pack. Keep it hot while you make the sauce.

Heat the butter, sage and garlic in a small saucepan. When the butter has just melted, add the cheese, cream and a good grinding of pepper.

Cook, stirring the whole time until the cheese has melted. Simmer for 1 minute. Taste and check if salt is needed; because of the saltiness of the cheese it probably will not be. Remove and discard the sage leaves, pour the sauce into a bowl, and serve with the freshly made polenta.

Polenta with pesto

Gluten-free/can be milk-free

Anna: *In Liguria, pesto is added to lasagne, layered with the local soft cheese. This dish uses polenta in the same way, and works really well.*

Michelle: *Those on milk-free diets might want to try this dish using one of the many new nut-based 'cheeses'. Alternatively, you could make it just with the pesto and the walnuts, both of which have lots of flavour of their own.*

Start by making the polenta following the instructions on the pack.

Pour the cooked polenta onto a wooden board, and spread it out to a thickness of 8mm. Allow to cool for at least 2 hours.

Preheat the oven to 200°C (400°F/fan 180°C/Gas 6). Grease a 25cm x 18cm baking dish – a lasagne dish is ideal – with 1 tablespoon of the olive oil.

When the polenta is cold, cut it into 2cm thick slices, and cover the base of the tin with approximately half of them. Season with pepper, drizzle with 1 tablespoon of the oil, then spread the pesto over the polenta pieces.

Set aside 2 tablespoons of the walnuts, and sprinkle the remainder over the pesto. Cover with half the mozzarella, torn into pieces, and half the Pecorino Romano. Layer the remaining polenta on top, sprinkle 1 tablespoon of the oil over it, and then top with the remaining mozzarella cut into slices.

Sprinkle with the remaining pecorino, walnuts and olive oil, and a generous grinding of pepper.

Cover the dish with foil and bake for about 20 minutes. Remove the foil and bake for a further 10 minutes until a lovely gold crust has formed on the top, and serve.

Serves 4–6

300g quick cook/instant polenta

freshly ground black pepper

4 tbsp extra virgin olive oil

250g Sacla' Free From Tomato Pesto (contains soya)

100g chopped walnuts

100g mozzarella (optional)

100g Pecorino Romano, grated (optional)

Chickpeas with rocket, chilli and garlic

Gluten-free/milk-free/lactose-free

Anna: *A simple, classic recipe from southern Italy, perfect for tinned chickpeas.*

Michelle: *And naturally milk-free too!*

Serves 4

4 garlic cloves

5 tbsp olive oil

1 fresh chilli, seeded and finely chopped

2 x 400g tins chickpeas, drained and rinsed

25–30g rocket

sea salt

a few tbsps gluten-free vegetable stock

freshly ground black pepper

Chop 2 of the garlic cloves very finely, and thread a wooden cocktail stick through the other 2 so that you can fish them out easily when the sauce is done (or if you like a very garlicky sauce, chop them all).

Heat the olive oil in a large sauté pan, add the garlic and the chilli and sauté for 1 minute. Add the chickpeas and gently heat them in the oil, turning them over and over so that they all get coated with the oil. Add 2 or 3 tablespoons of the stock to moisten them and cook for about 5–8 minutes, adding stock whenever necessary.

Put the rocket in a bowl and add the hot chickpea with all their juices. Fish out any whole garlic cloves and discard. Mix well, check the seasoning and add more salt if necessary, and serve warm or at room temperature with plenty of crusty gluten-free bread to mop up the juices.

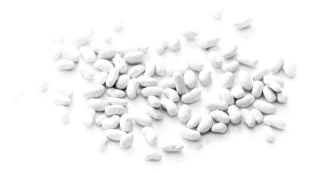

Cannellini beans with tomato and rosemary

Gluten-free/milk-free/lactose-free

erves 4

00ml extra virgin olive oil

2 fresh sage leaves, torn
to pieces

-3 garlic cloves, chopped

–1 tsp chilli flakes

x 400g tins cannellini
eans, drained and rinsed

00g ripe tomatoes, peeled
nd chopped

a salt

Anna: *This is a classic recipe from Tuscany, the region of the cannellini beans. It is one of the few recipes for pulses which are just as
good made with tinned beans. We hope you like it.*

Michelle: *This couldn't be simpler – or more delicious!*

Heat the olive oil in a frying pan and add the sage, garlic and chilli.
Fry for 1 minute, then throw in the beans. Sauté them gently for 2–3
minutes, while stirring constantly.

Add the tomatoes, salt to taste and continue cooking for about 10
minutes, then serve.

That's all; quick, easy and delicious.

Lentils with sausage and mushrooms

Gluten-free/milk-free/lactose-free

Serves 6

350g continental or green lentils

2 bay leaves

100g unsmoked pancetta cubes

4 tbsp olive oil

1 onion, finely chopped

1 celery stick, finely chopped

1 carrot, finely chopped

500g Italian Luganega or other coarse-grained, gluten-free pure pork sausages, skinned and cut into chunks

100ml red wine

400g can chopped plum tomatoes (with juice)

sea salt and freshly ground black pepper

1 garlic clove, peeled and lightly crushed

250g brown mushrooms, cleaned and sliced (or 1 jar Sacla' Free From Wild Mushroom Risotto – contains soya)

Anna: *An all-in-one meal, as delicious as it is nourishing. If you are pushed for time, Sacla' makes an excellent wild mushroom sauce that you could use instead of making the mushroom sauce.*

Michelle: *The original recipe was served with parmesan, but the dish has so much flavour that we really didn't think that it was needed.*

First, cook the lentils with the bay leaves and a little salt in plenty of boiling water for about 10 minutes. Reserve a mugful or so of the liquid, then drain the lentils.

In a large sauté pan, fry the pancetta in 1 tablespoon of the olive oil for 2 minutes, then add the onion, celery and carrot and continue frying until soft – about 7–8 minutes. Add the sausages and sauté for 5 minutes, breaking them up with a fork and turning them over and over so that they brown on all sides.

Pour over the wine, raise the heat, and boil fast for a minute or two. Add the tomatoes and their juice, and season. Stir, cover the pan and simmer for 30 minutes or so. If the sauce gets too dry during the cooking, add some of the lentil liquid.

Mix in the lentils and continue cooking, covered and over low heat, for some 20 minutes, stirring occasionally. Taste and adjust the seasoning.

While the sausage and lentils are cooking, make the mushroom sauce (or just heat the Sacla' Free From Wild Mushroom Risotto).

To make the mushroom sauce:

Put the remaining olive oil and the crushed garlic into a frying pan over low heat. When the oil hot, add the brown mushrooms and sauté for some 15 minutes, stirring frequently. Remove the garlic and discard, then add salt and pepper to taste.

Mix the mushroom sauce (whichever you are using) into the lentil mixture and cook all together for a couple of minutes, then serve.

Buckwheat polenta with butter and cheese

Gluten-free

Serves 4–5

250g buckwheat flour

125g polenta flour

2 tsp sea salt

150g unsalted butter cut into pieces
(plus extra butter for greasing)

300g Caerphilly, Wensleydale or
Lancashire cheese, cut into thin slices

a jar of Sacla' Truffle Pesto (optional –
contains milk, egg and cashew nuts)

grated parmesan to serve (optional)

Anna: *This is a speciality of the Alpine valleys that run between Lombardy and Alto Adige, where buckwheat grows plentifully. The polenta is made by substituting some buckwheat flour for polenta flour, thus producing a nuttier texture.*

In Italy we use a local cheese called Scimud. In the UK I use Caerphilly, Wensleydale and Lancashire, all of which have a similar texture and just a little of the tangy flavour needed. During the autumn, truffles are grated on top – a delicious treat. I have used the Sacla' Truffle Pesto instead, and it tastes excellent.

Michelle: *Another dish which depends entirely on the cheese and butter for its character, so it's impossible to make it milk-free!*

Heat the oven to 180°C (375°F/fan 160C/Gas 4). Heat 2.3 litres of water to just boiling point. Meanwhile, mix the two flours and the salt together.

When the water is nearly simmering (it will begin to form bubbles at the edge), draw the pan off the heat and add the two flours, fistful by fistful, letting it fall through your loosely closed fingers – while you beat the mixture in the pan hard with the other hand.

When all the flour has been added, put the pot back on the heat. Cook, beating constantly, until the mixture is bubbling hard like an erupting volcano.

Cook the polenta for 5 minutes, and then pour the mixture into a generously buttered oven dish that will amply contain the polenta. Cover with a piece of buttered foil, and bake for at least 1½ hours.

Remove the dish from the oven, turn the polenta into a large bowl, and beat in the butter, then the cheese. Continue to beat hard until both the cheese and butter have melted.

Top each portion with a teaspoon of Sacla' Truffle Pesto, if desired. Serve immediately with a bowl of grated parmesan on the side.

Soups

Broad bean soup p.50

Courgette soup

Gluten-free/can be milk-free

Serves 4

300g courgettes, cut into short matchsticks

1 banana shallot, peeled and chopped

25g unsalted butter (or 1 tbsp olive oil)

30ml olive oil

1.25 litres gluten-free chicken or vegetable stock

2 egg yolks

3 tbsp parmesan, grated

a pinch or two of grated nutmeg

2 tbsp double cream

sea salt and freshly ground black pepper

Anna: *This soup is a soft, pale green colour and is as attractive as it is delicious. The eggs added at the end of the cooking should curdle and thicken the broth.*

Michelle: *Although the classic version of this soup should be creamy, it actually is still lovely if you just leave out the cream and the parmesan and use an extra tablespoon of oil for cooking the courgette. Indeed, some would say that the flavour of the courgettes comes through even better, as it is not masked by the cream and the cheese!*

Place the courgettes in a colander, sprinkle with salt and leave to drain for 20–30 minutes. Dry them thoroughly with absorbent kitchen paper.

Put the shallot, butter and oil in a saucepan and cook gently until the shallot is translucent – but do not let it get brown or even gold. Add the courgette and sauté for 2–3 minutes, stirring all the time.

Pour in the stock, cover the pan and simmer for 15 minutes.

Gently beat together the egg yolks, cheese, nutmeg, cream and seasoning. Pour the mixture into the soup, stirring well. Boil for 1 minute, then serve at once.

Garlic soup

Gluten-free/can be milk-free/can be lactose-free

Anna: *The origin of this soup is half-French and half-Portuguese. The result is Italian, but it could be anywhere where garlic is used and loved. It seems to contain an awful quantity of garlic, but because it is properly cooked, the result is quite delicate.*

Michelle: *This is a delicious soup if you like garlic, so I was keen to find a milk-free way to make it. Using three tablespoons of a mild olive oil instead of the butter and oil, and four tablespoons of milk-free coconut yoghurt instead of the soured cream, seems to work pretty well.*

Serves 6

3 large red onions, chopped

2 sprigs thyme

either 50g unsalted butter and 3 tsp olive oil or 3 tbsp olive oil

sea salt

1 garlic bulb, peeled and chopped

3 large potatoes, cut into small cubes

2 bay leaves

3 tsp gluten-free vegetable bouillon powder

1 tbsp sour cream (or 4 tbsp milk-free coconut yoghurt)

a pinch of grated nutmeg

small bunch of chives, chopped

Gently fry the onion, and thyme in the butter and olive oil (or just the oil). Add a pinch of salt, cover with a lid and continue to fry gently, stirring frequently, until the onion is soft.

Add all the garlic and continue to cook slowly for 10 minutes, stirring frequently. Add the potatoes and the bay leaves and cook for 5 minutes. Mix in the bouillon powder and add 1 litre of boiling water, while stirring constantly. Simmer, covered, until the potatoes are done – it should take about 10 minutes.

Remove and discard the bay leaves and purée the soup with a stick blender; if it's too thick, add some more water. Mix in the sour cream (or coconut yoghurt) and nutmeg.

Taste, adjust the seasoning and ladle the soup into individual bowls. Sprinkle a little of the chives on top and serve.

Broad bean soup

Gluten-free/can be milk-free

Serves 4

1.5–1.75kg broad beans in their pods (or 300g podded or frozen broad beans, defrosted)

3 tbsp olive oil

1 large onion, cut into rings

1 garlic clove, sliced

500g ripe tomatoes, peeled and chopped

1.25 litres gluten-free vegetable stock

1 bay leaf

sea salt and freshly ground black pepper

2 level tbsp ricotta mixed with an equal amount of Sacla' Free From Tomato Pesto (contains soya). Or, if you want it to be milk-free, just use the tomato pesto

Anna: *The broad beans from central Italy are the best in the world; they are so tiny and sweet that, in Tuscany particularly, they are often eaten raw with local cheese, such as pecorino. Broad beans taste much better when peeled, but I leave that to you! You can also make the soup with frozen broad beans.*

Michelle: *A lovely filling and naturally freefrom soup – provided you leave out the optional ricotta cheese. (If you want the recipe to be milk-free, just use the tomato pesto). I do agree with Anna that the broad beans are much better peeled, especially as it is often hard to get them really young and tender in the UK.*

Remove the beans from their pods. If you are going to peel them, cook them for 1–2 minutes in boiling water, then remove them and plunge into cold water. After a couple of minutes, you will be able to break the skin on the end of the bean with a knife or your nail, and pop out the lovely green beans inside. Set them aside.

Heat the oil in a saucepan, add the onion and sauté until golden. Add the garlic, fry for a minute and then throw in the beans and fry for 30 seconds, stirring all the time.

Add the tomatoes and fry for a further 10 minutes, stirring frequently. Keep an eye on the pot and add a little stock if the tomatoes are getting burnt.

Pour in all the stock, add the bay leaf, cover and cook for about 7–8 minutes until the beans are tender. Taste and add salt and pepper.

Ladle the soup into individual bowls, and spoon some of the ricotta mixture (or the Sacla' Free From Tomato Pesto without the ricotta) into the middle of each bowl. Stir and serve.

Tuscan bean soup – La Ribollita

Gluten-free/milk-free/lactose-free

Serves 6

200g dried cannellini beans

100ml extra virgin olive oil

1 onion, finely chopped

1 carrot, chopped

1 celery stick, chopped

2 leeks, very finely sliced

2 ripe tomatoes, peeled, seeded and chopped

1 sprig of fresh rosemary, chopped

6 garlic cloves, peeled and finely chopped

1 sprig of fresh thyme

Flaked chilli, to taste

250g cavolo nero, stalks discarded and leaves finely sliced

sea salt and freshly ground black pepper

2 red onions, very finely sliced

2 tbsp Sacla' Free From Basil Pesto (optional – contains soya and cashew nuts)

Anna: *Ribollita means 'boiled again'. This Tuscan soup should be made at least a day in advance, in order to allow all the flavours to mingle and mix together. It is traditionally ladled on toasted bread, but it is also excellent without it.*

I am afraid tinned beans are not suitable for this soup because you need the flavour that the dried beans give to the liquid in which they are cooked. When cavolo nero is not in season, add a shredded romaine lettuce and leave out the onion topping. Just heat the soup, cook for 10 minutes and serve with a bowl of Sacla' Free From Basil Pesto for anybody who would like to dollop a little on the soup.

Michelle: *This soup is worth the effort of thinking ahead and soaking the beans – and it is naturally, totally freefrom!*

Soak the beans overnight. Drain and rinse them.

Choose a heavy stockpot (preferably earthenware) and put 2 tablespoons of the olive oil into it. Heat, add the onion, and after 5 minutes add the carrot, celery, leeks, tomatoes, rosemary and half the garlic.

Sauté for 10 minutes, stirring very frequently. Add the beans and turn them over and over to coat them in the oil. Cover with 2 litres of water, add salt and cook, covered, at the gentlest simmer for at least 2 hours, until the beans are very soft.

Lift out half of the beans and purée them in a food processor. Return the purée to the soup and stir well. Ideally the soup will now rest overnight, so you can cool and chill it at this point until you are ready.

Bring the soup back to a simmer, and preheat the oven to 180°C (375°F/fan 160°C/Gas 4).

Heat all but 1 tablespoon of the remaining oil in a small frying pan. Add the remaining garlic, thyme and chilli and sauté gently for about 2 minutes, stirring constantly and being very careful not to let the garlic burn.

Mix this into the soup, then add the cavolo nero. Taste and adjust the seasoning. Scatter the sliced red onion over the top of the soup. Mix the basil pesto with the remaining oil, and drizzle over the onion.

Place the soup in the oven for about ¾ to 1 hour, or until the onion is soft, and serve.

Other books by Anna Del Conte

If you would like to find out more about traditional and classical Italian cooking (much of it 'naturally' freefrom!) you should read some of Anna's other books.

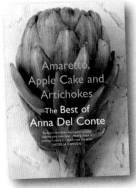

Anna first came to England in 1949 to work as an au pair. She was deeply shocked by British post-war food which was, as she said, 'not something you discussed but something you ate'. Despite the food, she did stay, married an Englishman and, once her children were older, started to write about 'real' Italian food. Her first book, *Portrait of Pasta*, came out in 1976 and was revised and republished in 2015 under a new title: *Anna Del Conte on Pasta*.

Other books followed but in the early 1980s she embarked on a massive encyclopaedia of Italian food and ingredients, the *Gastronomy of Italy* – everything you could ever want to know about Italian food from afrodisiaci and agnolotti to sfogliatelle and zuppa inglese! This was revised and republished in 2001 and again in 2013.

Other classic books appeared over the 1980s and 90s – among them the *Classic Food of Northern Italy* and *Entertaining all'Italiana*. But with the turn of the century she became a little more personal. *Amaretto, Apple Cake and Artichokes: The best of Anna Del Conte* appeared in 2006, *Risotto with Nettles: A Memoir with Food* in 2010 and Cooking with Coco: Family Recipes to Cook Together in 2011.

Finally this year, having finished her revision of her wheat-filled pasta book, she turned her mind to 'freefrom'!! And to a burgeoning television career!! A one-hour film about Anna's life in food was aired on BBC2 on December 16th!

Many of Anna's books have won prizes both in Italy and in the UK.

Other books by Michelle Berriedale-Johnson

If you would like to find out more about freefrom food and freefrom cooking, then you should look at the food and recipe pages on Michelle's FoodsMatter website – FoodsMatter.com. There are over 800 freefrom recipes – all free of gluten – 95% free of milk and 75% are free of nuts, soya, sesame and most of the other major allergens. Each recipe is flagged for what it is 'free of'. FoodsMatter also has huge directories of freefrom food manufacturers, mainly based in the UK.

Michelle has always been involved with food, first as a caterer in the 1970s and 80s and then as a historian of English food. She was just embarking on a major story on English food in the year that her son was diagnosed as dairy intolerant and she turned her attention to food allergies and intolerances. She had already written a number of books on food history (*Food fit for Pharoahs, The Victorian Cookbook, Pepys at Table, The British Museum Cookbook, Festive Feasts*) so it was not long before she was also writing for those on restricted diets: *Cooking Gluten, Wheat and Dairy Free, Diabetic Cooking for One or Two, The Everyday Wheat and Gluten Free Cookbook, Diabetic Cooking for Health, Eat to Beat IBS, Cooking for Arthritis* and more. The most recent to appear is her revised issue of her *The Allergy Catering Manual*, perfect for any catering establishment wanting to enter FoodsMatter's FreeFrom Eating Out Awards!